TWENTIETH-CENTURY DEVELOPMENTS IN FASHION AND COSTUME

MILITARY UNIFORMS

Other books in this series include:

Accessories
Carol Harris and Mike Brown

Children's Costumes
Carol Harris and Mike Brown

Women's Costumes
Carol Harris and Mike Brown

Men's Costumes
Carol Harris and Mike Brown

Festivals
Ellen Galford

North American Dress
Dr. Louise Aikman

Ceremonial Costumes
Lewis Lyons

Performing Arts
Alycen Mitchell

Everyday Dress
Chris McNab

Rescue Services
Carol Harris and Mike Brown

Religious Costumes
Ellen Galford

TWENTIETH-CENTURY DEVELOPMENTS IN FASHION AND COSTUME

MILITARY UNIFORMS

CAROL HARRIS AND MIKE BROWN

MASON CREST PUBLISHERS

www.masoncrest.com

Mason Crest Publishers Inc.
370 Reed Road
Broomall, PA 19008
(866) MCP-BOOK (toll free)
www.masoncrest.com

First printing 2002

1 2 3 4 5 6 7 8 9 10

Library of Congress Cataloging-in-Publication Data available

ISBN 1-59084-418-1

Printed and bound in Malaysia

Editorial and design by
Amber Books Ltd.
Bradley's Close
74–77 White Lion Street
London N1 9PF

Project Editor: Marie-Claire Muir
Designer: Zoe Mellors
Picture Research: Lisa Wren

Picture Credits:
Amber Books Ltd: 5 (all), 9, 11, 15, 18, 21, 24, 28, 33, 40, 42, 45, 46, 47, 49, 57. **TRH Pictures:** 6 (Peter Thrussell), 8, 10, 13 (Peter Thrussell), 14, 17 (Peter Thrussell), 20 (Peter Thrussell), 27, 31, 34, 35, 36, 37, 38-39 (Ian Loasby), 48, 50, 51, 52, 54, 58.

Cover images: TRH Pictures: (all) Main image: **TRH / Peter Thrussell**

Acknowledgment:
For authenticating this book, the Publishers would like to thank
JONES NEW YORK

Contents

Introduction

Every day we go to our closets with the same question in mind: what shall I wear today? Clothing can convey status, wealth, occupation, religion, sexual orientation, and social, political, and moral values. The clothes we wear affect how we are perceived and also reflect what image we want to project.

Fashion has always been influenced by the events, people, and places that shape society. The 20th century was a period of radical change, encompassing two world wars, suffrage, a worldwide Depression, the invention of "talkies" and the rise of Hollywood, the birth of the teenager, the global spread of television, and, later, the World Wide Web, to name just a few important developments. Politically, economically, technologically, and socially, the world was changing at a fast and furious pace. Fashion, directly influenced by all these factors, changed with them, leaving each period with its fashion icon.

The 1920s saw the flapper reign supreme, with her short dress and cropped, boyish hair. The '30s and '40s brought a wartime mindset: women entered the workforce en masse and traded their silk stockings for nylon. During the conservative 1950s—typified by twin sets and capri pants—a young Elvis Presley took the world by storm. The '60s gave us PVC, miniskirts, and mods, and in 1967, the Summer of Love spawned a new language of fashion in which bell-bottoms and tie-dyed shirts became political expressions of peace and love. In the 1980s, power and affluence became the hallmarks of a new social group, the yuppies. Designer branding led the way, and the slogan "Nothing comes between me and my Calvins" started an era of status dressing. The 1990s will be best remembered for a new fashion word introduced by the underground street and music movement of Seattle, grunge.

Twentieth-Century Developments in Fashion and Culture is a 12-volume, illustrated series that looks at changing fashions throughout this eventful century, and encourages readers to question what the clothes they wear reveal about themselves and the world they live in.

Special introduction and consultation:
JONES NEW YORK

CHAPTER 1

1900 – 1939

The early part of the 20th century saw fundamental changes in the colors and styles of uniforms, brought about by the need for better safety, comfort, and practicality. Out went bright, eye-catching uniforms and in came dull colors that helped hide fighting men from increasingly more effective weapons.

The last quarter of the 19th century and the opening of the 20th witnessed a great change in military uniforms that affected almost every country in the world. Before then, armies had gone to war gaudily dressed in brightly colored suits: the blues and the grays of the American Civil War, the British scarlet, French

Left, the cavalryman of the British Indian Army wears a distinctive turban. The *lungi*, or cloth that forms the turban, has stripes to denote his unit. The blue shirt and cowboy hat on this U.S. Army private from 1902 (right) are like those worn by "bluecoats" in the Indian wars.

blue, and a whole rainbow of oranges, purples, yellows, and greens, which made battlefields look like parades of toy soldiers. Today, this may seem silly, but at the time, it was a sensible solution to the problem of soldiers needing to quickly distinguish friend from foe.

In many cases, soldiers were not issued a full uniform, and those uniforms that did exist were usually tailor-made and thus, subject to a vast range of variations according to the whims of the tailor, the soldier, or his commanding officer. It was, therefore, necessary for each country to have some easily distinguishable mark—and what better than a coat, scarf, sash, or other item of clothing in a bright, easily recognizable color? Of course, the disadvantage was that soldiers were easily seen from a distance and were, therefore, easy targets for their enemies. In fact, the scarlet uniforms of the British in the American Revolution were so distinguishable that it led to their nickname: the Redcoats.

The growth of mass-production in factories meant that

From left to right are Belgian, French, and British soldiers of WWI. The French soldier wears a blue tunic with red trousers and collar patches. The buckle on the Englishman's belt was soon to be replaced.

soldiers in the same army could all be armed, equipped, and clothed in exactly the same manner, thus creating a uniform in the true sense of the word. As a result, soldiers no longer had to wear bright colors to recognize each other, and their uniforms could now be made in colors that blended into the background, usually browns, greens, and grays.

As with any change, there was resistance at first to these changes, especially among the more distinguished, older regiments. During the first two years of World War I, it was not uncommon to come across cavalrymen, especially in the German army, going into battle in bright regimental **tunics** and plumed helmets. However, by 1916, this practice had almost completely died out.

DRESS UNIFORMS

On a purely visual basis, the new uniforms were far less exciting than the ones that used bright colors, so the old uniforms were kept for use in parades and other ceremonial functions in which soldiers wanted to stand out. Soldiers always, if possible, kept a special uniform for this purpose, called a dress uniform, but it was usually just a newer, cleaner version of the uniform they fought in, with perhaps a little bit of extra gold braid on the shoulders or cuffs. Now, with the introduction of the new drab colors, the differences between combat dress and ceremonial uniforms were quite obvious.

Even today, many dress uniforms are descended from those worn by their 19th-century predecessors, such as the blue and

This German Uhlan officer of 1915 is notable for his distinctive helmet, here worn with a cloth cover, and the yellow (denoting cavalry) piping on his tunic, which is in the style called "lancer fronted."

white of the U.S. Marines, or the red coats and bearskin hats of Britain's Coldstream Guards.

However, another factor affected the way uniforms were changing: the new weapons that were being designed. In the first quarter of the 20th century, the biggest leaps forward in this respect were brought about by the massive conflict of World War I. Beginning as a war between Austria and Serbia in 1914, it soon spread to include most of Europe. By its end in 1918, forces from all around the globe were involved.

HELMETS, GAS MASKS, AND OTHER PROTECTION

The fighting in France, or the Western Front as it was called, soon became bogged down in a trench war, with both sides launching bombardments of shelling against each other. This included the use of shrapnel shells; these burst in the air, spraying a lethal hail of bullets onto the troops below. Before this war, soldiers in most armies wore some form of cloth headgear, such as the British **peaked cap**, the German peakless **pork-pie cap**, the U.S. cowboy-style **campaign hat**, and various **ski caps** and **side caps**.

The few helmets that were in use at this time were almost entirely worn for show rather than for protection. Good examples of this were the German *pickelhauben*, or spiked helmets. These were usually made mostly of leather or felt instead of metal, with a large brass badge on the front representing the wearer's unit, and different spikes showing the arm of service—a long spike for cavalry, a short spike for infantry, and a ball for artillery. In most cases, a cover made from the same cloth as the uniform was worn over the helmet for combat, and for ceremonial wear, a plume was added.

Cavalry units, such as the German Uhlans or the French lancers, wore many such ceremonial helmets, but beginning in 1916, soldiers on both sides tried to give themselves some sort of protection from shrapnel. At first, this was often in the form of a steel **skullcap** that was worn under the normal cap, especially by French troops. Later that year, soldiers on both sides were issued official steel or tin helmets, in a partial return to the armor worn during medieval times. These helmets could not deflect a bullet, but there were attempts to produce extra protection, such as a heavy steel shield that could be attached to the front of the German "coal scuttle helmet" for use by snipers. The heaviest helmets—and the most similar to their medieval predecessors—were those worn by some German storm troopers, who also wore **breastplates** and **chain mail** around their necks.

The use of chain mail was not exclusive to the Germans. Some British troops were issued with a chain mail curtain attached to the front of their helmets to make a face shield, but they were uncomfortable. Worse, their view was so restricted that many soldiers threw them away, so their issue was discontinued.

The use of poison gas against enemy troops was another development of World War I, first used by the Germans in Poland in January 1915. By the end of that year, both sides were using it, and this produced another piece of equipment to be added to the long list of items carried by the foot soldier: the gas mask. The first masks were primitive, like a surgical mask, and often worn with separate goggles, but these were soon improved. Gas masks limited the

The strange-looking helmet worn by this World War II German infantryman is, in fact, a standard spiked helmet with a field-gray cloth cover used in combat.

The German kaiser, or emperor (second from right), is shown with members of his high command. They wear a range of uniforms and headgear, and some carry ceremonial swords and daggers.

ability to see, and they made talking to other people difficult and impaired breathing—even when just sitting down—however, the protection they offered to soldiers from the deadly effects of gas was worth the discomfort.

It took time for the troops to get used to wearing gas masks, but soon, new recruits practiced fighting in them as part of their training. Troops in most armies continued to carry gas masks for the rest of the century, as the use of poison gas and other chemical weapons continued to pose a threat.

OFFICERS' UNIFORMS

Officers' uniforms were often tailor-made using good-quality cloth, which meant that they were extremely well fitting. They were often worn with long leather boots and belts. Other ranks' uniforms, produced in the hundreds of

This corporal from German East Africa clearly shows the sand-colored German tropical uniform. There is a cockade badge on the side of his broad-brimmed sun hat, and there are corporal's stripes on his left arm.

thousands, had to be both cheap and durable. They were usually made of woolen material, which was warm, but scratchy, especially when new. Unlike the officers' uniforms, they were generally a poor fit, although for many of the poorer **conscripts**, their uniform was the best suit they had ever owned.

The officer's jacket, or tunic, was usually worn open-necked with a shirt and tie, while those of other ranks were usually buttoned up to the neck. Tunics had to be capable of carrying a great many items, so it was common for them to have four large **pouch pockets**, with flaps and buttons to hold their contents securely. Loose trousers would quickly become caught and torn as troops moved over rough ground, so many armies at this time used puttees, strips of cloth that were wound around the leg from ankle to knee. Alternatives were the long **spats** used by some U.S. troops, or long leather boots, such as the dice shakers, worn by some units in the German army. Over all this was worn a large, heavy overcoat called a greatcoat. The coat, like the tunic, was fitted with shoulder straps or **epaulets**, which held the straps holding the equipment. In the winter, the greatcoat was augmented by nonofficially produced knitted items—a scarf, **balaclava helmet**, gloves, or mittens—often made by wives or sweethearts, although most countries organized collections of "comforts" for the troops.

CAVALRY

The machine gun had been in use for some time before World War I, but its use was perfected during this time. Machine guns were particularly effective against cavalry, wiping out the mounted troops before they could come to grips with their sabers and **lances**. Also, the trench warfare on the Western Front—bogged down with its barbed wire and mud-filled shell holes—made it almost impossible for horses to move freely across the battlefield.

Thus, World War I saw the end of the cavalry as a weapon of war in the West, and with them went their particular uniforms and equipment: riding breeches or **jodhpurs**, long riding boots, and, in the West, the sword. All these items, as well as the horse, largely disappeared from the battlefield to take their place in the dress parade.

The cavalry units themselves were converted to use the new "battle steed," the armored vehicle—in particular, the tank—another new development introduced by the British in 1916 in an unsuccessful attempt to break the deadlock of trench warfare.

Other additions included sleeveless leather **jerkins**, capes, and cloaks. Among Allied officers, a heavy, military-style, belted raincoat with epaulets was popular, and it became universally known as the trench coat.

BADGES OF RANK AND OTHER INSIGNIA

In a large army, it is necessary for a soldier's rank, and often his unit, to be easily seen. This was accomplished by the use of badges worn on the sleeves, epaulets, or collar, or by markings on the helmet. A system of stripes on the sleeve was common to many armies for **noncommissioned ranks**; the advantage of having stripes on the sleeve was that they were visible from almost any angle.

Officers were immediately recognizable by their superior uniforms, and often by their hats, which were almost always different from those of the lower ranks. However their actual rank was signified by systems of bars, **pips**, crowns, crossed swords, and so on, often worn on the epaulets. Variations included, for example, the British use of markings on the cuff, which was used at the beginning of the war, although by 1917, it was rapidly being replaced by epaulet markings. The main reason for this was the rapidly increasing accuracy and range of the rifle. With this came the sniper, who was trained to target first the officers, then the noncommissioned officers.

The answer to this was a rank system that could be seen easily at close range, but not at a distance. For this reason, badges in browns and greens, which, from a distance, would blend in with the uniform, replaced the intricate, brightly colored, braid rank badges. The same applied to specialist badges—such as those for medics, electricians, carpenters, **farriers**, artillery, and so on—and unit badges, usually worn on the sleeve or the epaulets.

A British second lieutenant (left) is shown with a corporal (right). The officer wears an open collar and tie, peaked cap, and Sam Browne belt.

PERSONAL KIT

The "modern" soldier was to be self-sufficient, which meant that as well as carrying his gun, he had to carry enough ammunition for a fairly long skirmish; a **bayonet**; an entrenching tool (a shovel or pick); food; water; a blanket; some spare clothing, including a greatcoat; and other items, such as field **dressings**, personal gear, grenades, and a gas mask. Nonofficial items included trench knives, **coshes**, clubs, and homemade, sharpened shovels for hand-to-hand fighting. Altogether, this could weigh up to 80 pounds (36 kg).

This posed several problems. Part of the answer was a good kit bag, or knapsack, but some of the gear had to be easily accessible, such as the ammunition and the gas mask. Some items, such as the ammunition, the bayonet, pistol, and the entrenching tool, were hung from the soldier's belt, but these weighed a lot—the British ammunition pouches, for instance, carried 100 bullets. All this extra weight often dragged the belt down.

The answer was found in suspenders: a leather arrangement was used to hold up the belt, and, by passing through the epaulets, it kept everything neatly in place while transferring the load to the shoulders. Separate bags were used to carry such items as a water bottle, gas mask, or grenades, and these, too, were passed through the epaulets.

WOMEN IN UNIFORM

By 1916, shortages of able-bodied men were creating problems for the British army, which began to use women to release men for active service. In July 1917, the Army High Command authorized the formation of the Women's Auxiliary Army Corps (WAAC).

This British second lieutenant wears a tank uniform, with puttees on his legs, rank pips on his cuffs, short pants, and a chain mail face protector—an idea that proved impractical.

SPECIALIST UNIFORMS

Some specialist units developed special items of clothing. The rapidly expanding flying units, for instance, wore tunics with no visible buttons, as well as leather coats and hats to protect against the bitter cold they experienced in their open cockpits. Tank crews, too, were often issued with leather clothing and special helmets.

In what was truly a worldwide war, battlefield conditions varied, from the bitter cold of the Russian front to the oppressive heat of Gallipoli in Turkey, and uniforms reflected these widely varying temperatures. In many cases, soldiers serving in extremes of cold were issued with special fur-lined coats, boots, and hats, while for those serving in hotter countries, a **tropical kit** was issued. This was usually made from a far thinner material than the normal uniform, and it often included a wide-brimmed hat to give some protection from the beating sun. French troops of the famous Foreign Legion wore a hat called a kepi, which had a loose piece of material hanging down at the back to protect the wearer from sunstroke.

Their main duties were administrative, clerical, domestic, and as drivers. Over 57,000 "Tommettes" were enrolled (men were called "Tommies"), including 1,000 who worked with the American Expeditionary Force.

Members wore a long, one-piece, single-breasted coatdress of **khaki** gabardine with a beech-brown collar, fastened by a belt of similar material. The coatdress, a kind of overall, had two flapped and buttoned pockets at hip level. The hemline was 12 inches (30 cm), an almost scandalously short length in 1917. This was worn with a broad-brimmed hat in khaki, with a brown hatband, and the WAAC badge on the front. In bad weather, the women also wore a single-breasted, belted khaki raincoat.

CHAPTER 2

World War II Allied Forces

Military weapons, tactics, and uniforms all tend to develop rapidly during periods of conflict and to remain fairly stable during times of peace. This was certainly true of the period between the two world wars.

When World War II began in Europe in 1939, the uniforms and equipment worn and carried by the soldiers were, in many cases, not much different from those their fathers had worn in 1918.

This 1940s' British infantryman (right) wears special snow clothing—a piece of early camouflage. The suit is padded and double-breasted for protection against the cold. The British paratrooper (left) wears a red beret.

Once again, a major war led to great improvements in the design of military uniforms. The mass slaughter of World War I had caused such outcries among the public that care of the men became a major concern for military planners. Uniforms were designed that offered greater protection from the elements and better blending into the background. The two biggest changes that took place during this time were the evolution of uniform variations for specialist troops and the development of **camouflage**.

GREAT BRITAIN AND THE COMMONWEALTH

The Tommy's uniform had seen several changes since 1918, although the men were still recognizable as British soldiers. Uniforms were still in khaki, but the tunic was different. Whereas before it had been a thigh-length jacket with four pouch pockets, it was now waist-length, in a style called a **blouson**, with two chest pockets. The sleeves were now button-fastened at the wrist, like a shirt, making them far warmer and more waterproof. This style of tunic gave the wearer much more freedom of action and was generally well liked by the troops.

In action, virtually all soldiers of any rank wore the blouson tunic, even including field marshals, such as Montgomery. All junior officers wore it—which, combined with small rank badges, made the task of picking out officers much more difficult for snipers.

Puttees, the bindings covering the legs, had disappeared, much to the troops' relief, because they took a long time to put on properly. They were replaced by gaiters, a simple piece of canvas that wrapped around the bottom of the trousers at the ankle, fastened easily and quickly by two buckles.

The leather jerkin continued to be popular, and the helmet was also virtually the same. Other things were different. For other ranks, peaked caps were largely replaced by **berets**, either black or khaki. For the most part, officers still wore the peaked cap, but it was not uncommon for them to wear a beret in combat. Leather for belts and straps had been completely replaced by a woven fabric

CAMOUFLAGE

The greatest change in military uniforms in this period was in the use of camouflage. This was a logical extension of the dull coloring of uniforms, but had not been widely used up to this point. Some German storm troopers in World War I had painted their steel helmets in a broken combination of greens, yellows, and browns—an idea that had originally been used on ships, tanks, and aircraft to counter the growing efficiency of aerial surveillance.

The first use of camouflaged cloth was in 1929, when the Italian army introduced its use for tents. One year later, the Germans used the idea for a dual-purpose item that was both a **poncho** and a section of a tent. In this way, the first piece of camouflaged uniform was born.

The Germans continued to develop camouflaged uniforms, but, as with any good idea, it was soon copied. By the end of the war, most countries' forces were at least partially dressed in camouflage items.

called **webbing**. Today, this term applies to any system of belts, straps, and pouches, regardless of the material.

The new uniform proved to be far more practical and comfortable than its predecessor, and so was quite popular with the troops. However, it was much less popular with retired generals and colonels, many of whom complained that it was scruffy and unmilitary.

Snow and Tropical Kits

World War II was a wide-ranging conflict, thus, there were extremes of temperature and conditions, and uniforms reflected this in their coloring. The winter of 1939–1940, for instance, was a snowy one on the Belgian front, where most British forces were stationed. They were issued white snowproof overalls and helmet covers, so they could blend into the background.

After the fall of France in June 1940, the main action moved to North Africa. Troops there mostly wore a tropical kit of shirts and shorts—often with long socks—in a sandy color. The same outfits were worn by British troops stationed in such places as Singapore and Hong Kong. In the desert battlefields, uniform rules were relaxed, with soldiers on both sides wearing nothing but shorts, and at times, it was confusing to know who was who.

Special Forces

In the desert, British tank officers took to wearing suede shoes, corduroy trousers, and short-sleeved cardigans (thus giving birth to the first "tank top"). Tank troops were often dressed in oil-stained overalls, giving rise to the complaint that they looked more like mechanics than soldiers—but, in fact, that is exactly what they were.

British commando units were trained to fight in all conditions, and their uniforms reflected this. For mountain or Arctic warfare, thick, padded, waterproof overalls were developed. The "cap comforter" was another commando development: a woolen cap that could be worn under the helmet, and also be pulled down to form a balaclava helmet. Other commando kit included rubber-soled boots, for silence, and the famous commando knife.

This Gurkha corporal (1941) wears British tropical dress, with Gurkha badges, a slouch hat, and a *kukri*—a vicious, curved, combat knife. The buttons on the legs of his shorts allow the length to be adjusted.

British paratroopers, a new form of specialist soldier formed in 1940, also wore camouflaged clothing. They wore trousers and a long overall top called a smock, both camouflaged. Their helmets were close fitting and brimless to make jumping easier and less hazardous. Their deep-red berets inspired their nicknames: Red Berets or Red Devils.

Women in Uniform

During World War II, Britain had half a million women in uniform. These included the Women's Royal Naval Service (WRNS), the Women's Auxiliary Air Force (WAAF), and the Auxiliary Territorial Service (ATS). British women played a much more active role in warfare than those of other countries. Many worked in traditional roles, such as nursing, or worked as clerical staff, wireless operators, and so on, but others operated searchlights and even manned antiaircraft guns. Their uniforms reflected these roles, from the **walking-out dress** of the clerical staff, through mechanics' overalls, to full **battle dress** for antiaircraft crews.

Service dress consisted of a long, tailored, four-pocket tunic similar to those of male officers, worn open-necked over a shirt and tie, with a calf-length skirt, all in khaki. Worn with this was a side cap or, more commonly, a special peaked cap, a double-breasted greatcoat, and thick khaki stockings made of a material called lisle. If a woman was lucky enough to get one that fitted properly, the uniform could look stylish and feminine.

ATS motorcycle dispatch riders wore breeches and puttees, while for mechanics, a one-piece green denim overall was produced. Antiaircraft crews wore battle dress consisting of a blouson jacket similar to the one wore by the men—although of better-quality fabric—along with slacks, ankle boots, and short leather gaiters.

In cold weather, all ATS uniforms might be worn with the ever-popular leather jerkin. Antiaircraft work was often cold work, so ATS gun crews were issued with a special "wool pile" overcoat, a sort of fake fur garment popularly known as the "teddy bear coat." With this, they wore the standard steel helmet.

ATS personnel served in all the main theaters of war, so there were tropical versions of ATS uniform: a lightweight, sand-colored skirt, shirt, tunic, and service cap, or a jungle-green version with a slouch hat.

Another group of army women, the army nurses, wore nurses' uniforms on the wards, but for walking-out dress, they wore uniforms similar to the ATS, including battle dress and tropical versions.

Commonwealth Troops

With the British forces came hundreds of thousands of **Commonwealth** troops from India, Africa, Canada, Australia, the West Indies, and dozens of other countries throughout the world. They were nearly all dressed in British uniform, the main differences being the hats they wore (for example, Sikh turbans and Australian slouch hats) and sometimes their weapons (such as **Gurkha kukris**). One very British ethnic uniform was the **kilt** and **tam-o'-shanter** worn by Scottish regiments; in World War I, the Germans at first treated them as a joke, but soon learned better, dubbing them the "ladies from hell."

FRANCE, BELGIUM, AND THE "FREE" FORCES

In 1935, France had introduced a khaki uniform to replace the traditional blue, although many units retained a blue cap, or kepi. However, the basic uniform still resembled that of 1918, with a long, waisted, single-breasted tunic, riding-type breeches or baggy **pantaloons**, puttees, and leather webbing. With this was worn the familiar French *poilu* helmet, which was used by several other countries, including Switzerland and Spain. Officers' uniforms were of a similar style to the men's, although they were usually of far superior cut and material. The other main difference was the use of brown riding boots or long leather gaiters instead of puttees.

French specialist forces included armored troops, who were issued with a three-quarter-length brown leather coat, loose gabardine trousers, and a blue beret. French tank troops were issued with a special helmet designed for protection and comfort in the hot, cramped interior of a tank.

Noncommissioned officers and men of the Belgian army wore uniforms that were heavily influenced by the French, although their soldiers wore long leather gaiters instead of puttees. Their officers' uniforms, however, were based on the British pattern, with peaked cap, **Sam Browne belt**, long leather boots, riding breeches, and a long, four-pocket tunic worn open-necked over shirt and tie.

Czechoslovakia fell to the Germans in March 1939, but before that—and in some cases after—there had been a flood of Czechs into the west, usually to France. After the war broke out in September of that year, France formed a Czech division from the refugees. This was the first of many such units, as countries fell to the invading Germans and

These U.S. soldiers are wearing the classic M1941 that came into popular use during World War II.

those who could sought refuge with their allies. The uniform of the Czech division was typical in that it was almost entirely that of the host nation, in this case France, with Czech **insignia**.

The same happened to the French themselves. French, Belgian, Dutch, Norwegian, Polish, Czech, and other soldiers made their way to Britain, where "free" forces, such as the Free French, were set up. As expected, their new uniforms were sometimes—but not always—those of the British, with their own badges to denote their unit and rank. Whenever possible, the Free French continued to wear *poilu* helmets and their officers wore kepis, but there are many cases of Free French units wearing British or U.S. helmets.

THE UNITED STATES

For most countries, there was little development of military uniforms during peacetime. This was particularly true of the U.S. When it entered the war in December 1941, many of its soldiers were equipped with uniforms, kit, and weapons that were not just similar to those worn by their fathers in 1917, but were actually the same.

This U.S. Marine from 1943 is in a standard Marine herringbone twill uniform. The sword and the water bottle at his front are, in fact, Japanese issue; his own water bottle can be seen on the right.

New Uniforms

In 1917, the classic M1941 helmet was introduced. This replaced the previous 1917-issue wide-brimmed helmet, based on the British pattern. However, for at least two years after Pearl Harbor, it was common to see American troops wearing the early model. One unusual feature of American helmets was the custom of painting the wearer's rank on the front of the helmet, making the sniper's job that much easier. The Germans and French had unit insignia on their helmets, but in most armies, the only markings on combat helmets would be red crosses signifying medical orderlies, hopefully to spare them from the sniper's attention. Another piece of U.S. headgear that had survived from earlier uniforms was the broad-brimmed campaign hat, popular with cavalry regiments and especially noncommissioned officers.

Another change made in the early 1940s was the replacement of leather webbing with woven material, the belts of which had **eyelets** around them for attaching ammunition pouches, holsters, and other such things. The old laced **anklets** were replaced by elasticized versions, making life easier for the troops. Eventually, these, too, were replaced by high-laced boots originally designed for airborne units.

America's Army and Marine Corps uniforms came in two basic colors: khaki and olive drab. Khaki was meant for tropical wear and olive for other use, although it was common to see combinations of both. After their poor start, great changes were made. From 1943 on, the U.S. Army was issued with uniforms far superior to its allies and made with new materials, lightweight yet waterproof. One example was the field jacket, the 1941 model being made of light tan, windproof cotton with a wool flannel lining in a design based on the civilian windbreaker jacket. At first, this proved popular with the troops; with its zipper front, it was both comfortable and practical. But two major drawbacks soon became evident. First, it did not keep its wearer warm in field use and, second, it quickly wore out.

Its 1943 successor was longer and featured a drawstring waist and a hood and collar that could be buttoned at the neck for extra protection from the cold. Another feature was four large pockets for carrying small items, including ammunition and food. It was sometimes worn under a special combat vest that had built-in ammunition pockets. There were also matching trousers that could be worn over the normal wool trousers in cold weather. This established a new trend in uniform design: several thin layers instead of one thick item—a more efficient way of keeping in the heat. This idea more than proved itself during the bitter weather of the Battle of the Bulge in the winter of 1944. One offshoot of that winter was the makeshift snow camouflage, in which troops made ponchos and helmet covers from white bed sheets and pillowcases.

There was also a noncombat uniform that was not a dress uniform. The Germans called this a "walking-out uniform." For American troops, it took the form of a full-length olive-drab tunic of the four-pocket style worn over a khaki shirt and olive-drab tie, and trousers, usually in khaki, with anklets and boots. This was finished off with a side cap and belt. What made other Allied troops envious of this was the superior materials and cut; the British battle dress might have been practical, but it took a lot of work to make it look halfway stylish.

In 1944, a new jacket was introduced, similar in design to the British battle dress, but vastly superior in cut and material. Produced in dark olive-drab, it soon became known as the **Ike jacket**, named for General Dwight "Ike" Eisenhower. It was produced for either combat or walking-out wear, but most troops kept it purely for the latter.

Tankwear

The tank might have offered a great deal of protection for its crew, but inside it was cramped and could become extremely hot. This, and the rough ground over which a tank was expected to move, meant that getting a serious bang on the head was always a danger. Another great danger was "brewing up"—in other words, being hit by an antitank shell and catching fire. If this happened, the crew had only seconds to escape through narrow hatches—in which event loose buttons and equipment could be a real hazard, because they increase the danger of getting snagged; so tank uniforms were often lightweight and simple.

An American (rear center) is teaching Chinese troops to use a machine gun. Note the lack of insignia on the Chinese uniforms and their use of puttees to protect their lower legs. The U.S. instructor is wearing a bush hat or slouch hat.

American tank crews were issued with belted, **herringbone** twill overalls in olive. Especially popular was the tank crew jacket. This was made of lightweight khaki, waist-length, and elasticized at the waist and sleeves, with two large slash pockets and a knitted collar. Another item of tank uniform was the special lightweight helmet, made from fiber instead of metal, light yet still strong. It had a series of holes drilled in the top to increase ventilation.

Tropical and Specialist Uniforms

For tropical wear, shirts, trousers, and ties were issued that were made from a khaki drill material called chino in the U.S. These were worn with a distinctive narrow webbing belt with a plain, gilt-finish belt plate.

For the war in the Pacific, the U.S. Marines were issued with a two-piece herringbone twill uniform and matching peaked **forage cap**, all in olive-drab. The jacket had a single breast pocket with the Marines' badge stenciled on it. There was a less-popular **dungaree** version. Marines' helmets were often fitted with a camouflaged cover in one of several patterns.

Other specialist troops included the airborne divisions. They had their own uniform, a two-piece, olive-green tunic and trousers. The trousers had reinforced knees to protect their joints on landing. Another weak point on landing was the paratrooper's ankles. It was found that tightly laced boots that covered the ankle gave the men extra protection, so they were issued with these instead of the normal anklets. U.S. airborne troops did not have a special helmet like their British and German counterparts—they used the standard M1941 helmet with a special lining and chin strap.

Women in Uniform

American women could join the WAACs or nursing teams, including the American Red Cross. Apart from nursing, however, their duties were mainly administrative and clerical.

As with all later U.S. uniforms, the women's walking-out uniform was extremely stylish and well-tailored in dark brown, olive-drab, or chino, consisting of a knee-length skirt and a long, two-pocket tunic over a shirt and tie, worn with a peaked or side cap. Nursing **fatigues** were a two-piece overall of loose shirt and trousers in khaki denim, worn with a dark baseball cap or **bush hat**.

U.S.S.R.

Soviet troops wore a long, khaki, four-pocket tunic with a high collar. Both officers and other ranks wore breeches or trousers with long leather boots and webbing. These could be worn with a side cap, a fur-lined winter cap with large earflaps, or the Soviet-style helmet, similar to the American version. Officers wore a peaked cap, the dress version of which was broader than normal. Over all this could be worn the long, double-breasted greatcoat. Rank was indicated by epaulets worn on both the tunic and the greatcoat. (Soviet epaulets were larger than those of most other countries.)

The Soviet troops were particularly well equipped for the vicious conditions of the Russian winter, with snow smocks, fur hats, and felt boots.

Russian women fought in the frontline, and they were excellent snipers. This Soviet woman sniper from 1943 wears a one-piece camouflaged coverall, with baggy cap and hood to break up her silhouette.

CHAPTER 3

World War II Axis Forces

Both Germany and Italy took pride in their stylish uniforms, but as warfare became more sophisticated and varied, there arose a corresponding need for innovations in clothing and equipment.

Under the Treaty of Versailles, which brought an end to World War I, Germany had to get rid of most of her armed forces. Then, in March 1935, Hitler announced that he was reintroducing **conscription**. His new army needed to be equipped and clothed, and, unlike its Allied counterparts, its uniforms were to be new and up-to-date.

The black uniform on the officer (left) has the pink piping and skull-and-crossbones collar patches of the panzer, or armored troops; the German eagle shows that he is army, not SS. The soldier (far right) has the cuff band of the elite Herman Göring Division.

Certainly, at the beginning of the war between the Axis and Allied countries, German uniforms were the most stylish and best-cut in the world, but as the war dragged on, new versions were brought out that were increasingly badly cut and made of poorer material. Troops were soon issued with whatever uniforms were available, including Italian-issue clothing, so that men of the same unit were often dressed in a whole range of uniform styles and colors.

These German paratroopers are wearing a typical uniform—light-gray air force side caps, baggy khaki trousers, and air force ground-personnel field coat in splinter camouflage. A paratrooper helmet, center, has a netting cover.

Hitler is shown with paratroopers in 1940. They are wearing the early para-smock and para-helmet, with camouflage cover. There is a selection of iron crosses, including the Knight's Cross, around the neck.

THE STANDARD GERMAN UNIFORM

The uniform blouse was still a long, four-pocket tunic in field gray, but lightweight and better tailored. It still had a dark stand-and-fall collar (one that could be worn either buttoned to the neck or open, like a sports jacket) on which regimental badges were worn, with noncommissioned officers' ranks shown on the sleeve, as well as trade badges, such as driver. Epaulets showed officers' ranks and, in some cases, the wearer's unit. The one big difference in insignia from 1918 on was the Nazi eagle and swastika worn above the right breast pocket.

For cold weather, a greatcoat was issued. This was double-breasted, calf-length, and waisted. Like the tunic, the greatcoat was in field gray with a darker collar. Unlike many other armies, it was not issued with a belt. If one was required, the normal-service leather belt was worn. No insignia, other than rank badges, was worn on the greatcoat. An alternative, worn almost exclusively by officers, was a long leather overcoat in green, gray, or black. Once again, rank epaulets were worn with it.

New helmets, introduced in 1935, were a smaller version of the original 1917 coal scuttle. Painted green or black, they usually had shield-shaped insignia on the sides: a red, white, and black tricolor on the left, and an eagle and swastika on the right. There were variations. The SS had its own symbol on the right and a swastika on the left. Helmets might be covered with a camouflaged cloth cover or chicken wire, to which could be attached pieces of greenery or other similar items for camouflage. The pork-pie cap was replaced by either a side cap or a ski cap for enlisted men and noncommissioned officers. Officers also wore these, but more commonly, a peaked cap.

There are SS collar patches on the tunics, worn under the camouflage smocks, of these SS infantry troops. Between them they are wearing at least four different camouflage variations on smocks, pants, or helmet covers.

All troops continued to wear leather webbing, the main difference in the belt being the buckle, which in World War I had been brass. These new steel buckles were painted green or gray, so they would not reflect the light. Officers were issued with a circular buckle, but as these came undone easily, many officers opted to wear the ordinary version, especially in combat. Leather was also used for the other ranks' calf-length leather boots, known as dice shakers.

One easily recognizable piece of equipment was the gas mask, which had a cylindrical, corrugated-steel case, unlike most other armies, which used cloth bags. One of the most innovative pieces of equipment was the poncho, or *zeltbahn*—a triangle of camouflaged, waterproof material. Four of these ponchos could be secured together to form a four-man tent, provided one soldier could find three others.

This Italian tank man, in North Africa in 1941, is wearing a functional tank uniform. It includes a leather crash helmet with neck protector, leather overcoat, and loose-fitting pants.

Armored Troops

German panzer (armored) units had a distinctive uniform. The blouson top—suitable for sitting in a cramped tank— was double-breasted with concealed buttons. The trousers were baggy, for coolness and comfort, and worn with short ankle boots. They also wore a padded beret to protect the head. Alternatives to the beret were the side cap, the ski cap, or, for officers, the peaked cap. Particularly distinctive was the fact that the whole uniform was in black, which, with the panzer regiments' skull-and-crossbones **collar patches**, often led to confusion between them and the SS. The main distinguishing point was that the panzer regiments wore the normal army eagle and swastika on their right breast. To finish off the uniform, they wore a gray shirt and black tie and the army-style belt in black.

Panzer **grenadier** assault gun units wore a uniform of similar cut, but in field gray. They did not, however, wear the beret.

Tropical Uniforms

The German Afrika Korps wore a tunic based on the pattern of the normal uniform, but in lightweight khaki, almost always worn open-necked. Trousers were loose and straight, or else breeches were worn. Shorts were also used, but less often than among the British. The normal leather belt, usually in brown, completed the outfit, although there were woven-cloth versions. Originally, they were issued with high, suede, lace-up boots, but in the arid heat of the desert, these proved unpopular and were soon rejected in favor of ankle boots.

As with the Allied troops, desert heat meant that uniform rules were more relaxed. Panzer troops wore "normal" tropical uniforms, while most officers wore the tropical ski cap. Soon, most soldiers on both sides looked similar, with an open-necked shirt or **singlet** with shorts or loose trousers. One of the few ways to distinguish between them was the steel helmet. The German version was painted sand-colored, often with the Afrika Korps insignia stenciled on—a palm tree on top of a swastika. **Pith helmets** were also worn, bearing metal versions of the tricolor and eagle and swastika shields.

Paratroopers

German paratroop regiments were first used in combat for the invasion of Crete in 1941. Due to their extremely high casualty rate, however, they were never used again in a mass drop, but Winston Churchill was so impressed by them that Britain set up its own parachute regiments.

Paratroopers' helmets had to be compact to avoid snagging on the supporting ropes of the parachute, yet give protection in case of a heavy landing. The jackets also needed to be simple, while providing good insulation against the cold encountered at high altitudes. German paratroopers were issued with a special, pot-shaped helmet bearing the German tricolor and the special air force eagle and swastika. They wore normal combat uniforms, over which they wore a jump smock with a zipper for easy removal. Early versions were in khaki, but these were soon replaced by a field-gray version, which was, in turn, replaced by a camouflage version in 1941.

To protect their knees when landing, they wore special, **kapok**-filled knee pads over their trousers. The outfit was completed with rubber-soled ankle boots and a **Luftwaffe** belt, whose buckle was longer than the army version and bore the air force eagle and swastika.

After Crete, paratroopers were used almost exclusively as ground troops, so their special equipment was increasingly replaced by normal combat uniforms. They continued to wear the paratrooper helmet, often with the smock replaced by the knee-length Luftwaffe camouflaged field coat.

Mountain Troops

German mountain troops wore normal combat uniforms, almost exclusively with ski caps, upon the side of which they wore the Alpine **edelweiss** badge in metal. A similar cloth badge was worn on the right arm. The basic outfit was finished off with heavy ankle-length boots, and these were usually worn with a pair of short gaiters to give extra protection to the ankles.

In winter, they would wear a hooded **anorak** over the uniform, often with matching trousers. Both of these were reversible, often with field gray or normal camouflage on one side and plain white on the other. These were widely used by units on the Russian front, but conditions there were so bad that all sorts of clothing were worn to try to keep out the extreme cold. This included civilian fur coats, Russian felt boots, and straw boot covers.

This Blackshirt corporal is wearing the standard gray-green Italian uniform, but with fascist black shirt and tie, Blackshirt collar patches and helmet badge, and the specially designed Blackshirt dagger.

The SS

The Schutzstaffel, or SS—the Nazi party militia—grew to such huge proportions that it formed its own fighting regiment: the Waffen SS. They wore standard combat uniforms, but with SS badges instead of army ones. These mainly took the form of rectangular black collar patches, the right one bearing the SS insignia and the left, the wearer's rank. The other main difference from the army uniform was a special eagle and swastika worn on the upper-left sleeve instead of on the right breast. The SS had its own armored grenadier, and mountain troops, who all wore the particular uniforms of those forces, but with SS badges.

The SS pioneered the use of camouflaged clothing. Several outfits were designed to be worn over the normal uniform, usually with smock tops, but a waist-length version was also provided for tank crews. Camouflage design became more of an art form, and several different patterns were produced for different conditions, including the early "splinter," "palm tree," "plane tree," "pea," and "oak leaf" patterns.

Women in Uniform

German women were supposed to devote themselves to *kinder, kirche, kuche* (children, church, and kitchen), yet some single women were allowed into uniform as nurses or for administrative or clerical duties. Nazi ideology meant that they were never allowed to become as directly involved in the war as the British ATS, or even the U.S. WAACs. Nazi uniforms were stylish in cut and design: a long, tailored tunic and skirt in field gray, worn open-necked over a white shirt and gray tie, and finished with a side cap.

ITALIAN UNIFORMS

Italian uniforms were designed to glorify the military, and even nonmilitary organizations were dressed in martial outfits. Under Mussolini, uniforms—

both military and civilian—proliferated in Italy. Flamboyant outfits were made for high civil officials, or, in the military, for dress uniforms, yet in **fascist** Italy, this love of uniform was often combined with classic Italian style.

Combat uniforms were far less flashy, yet—at least during the first half of the war—were designed and well tailored. The principal color of Italian army uniforms was gray-green. The coat was a long, four-pocket tunic, similar to that of the Germans, worn open-necked with a gray-green shirt and tie. If conditions warranted, a loose blue sweater could be worn instead of (or sometimes over) the tunic. Officers' tunics were of a similar style, but made of a lighter-colored material of a far superior quality and tailoring, worn with a white shirt and gray tie.

Other ranks' trousers were lighter in color than the tunic, cut loosely and worn with long gaiters or puttees. Broader, thicker trousers, called pantaloons, were also worn. Officers wore breeches with long black leather boots, in contrast to other ranks' boots, which were ankle-length in brown or black.

Webbing was of leather or woven material, usually in black or gray, although officers' Sam Browne-style belts were usually brown. The helmet was a cross between the American and Russian styles, in dark gray. Caps came in a range of styles. Some officers wore peaked caps, but the most common style for both officers and men was the side cap, often with a tassel at the front.

Tropical Dress

Italian tropical uniform was designed for comfort in the extreme heat: either khaki shorts with long socks, or loose trousers with suede ankle-boots. As usual, officers mostly wore khaki breeches and riding boots. All ranks wore a tunic called the *sahariana*, which was extremely well-made of a light drill material in the style of the normal tunic. This was a popular item, and not only with the Italians— they would be seen on any German or British troops who could manage to get hold of them. For the colder nights, a khaki version of the sweater was produced.

Tank Troops

Like Allied tank crews, Italian armored units wore clothes adapted for comfort in the hot, narrow confines of a tank, instead of for style. A light, loose tunic and trousers, worn without gaiters or puttees, were the main items of uniform. These were worn with a special tank-crew helmet, similar to the army motorcycle crash helmet: pot-shaped and made of leather, with a padded strip around the edge for added protection. To this could be added a leather neck protector, like the curtain worn by members of the French Foreign Legion. For cold or wet weather, a knee-length leather overcoat was issued, usually in black or dark gray.

Paratroopers

Italy was one of the pioneers in the use of parachute forces. Its first paratroopers began training in the late 1920s. Their uniforms were similar to the British and German equivalents: a knee-length camouflaged smock, with loose, comfortable trousers, over which was worn padded knee protectors. The helmet was the familiar pot-shaped paratroop style, usually painted in a camouflage pattern, with the normal heavy-duty chin strap used by paratroopers and motorcycle dispatch riders.

This corporal is of the Italian North African colonial forces. He is wearing a white-dress version of the *sahariana* jacket with baggy khaki pants.

The Blackshirts

The Italian fascist party had its own militia, the Milizia per la Sicurezza. Because this name was quite a mouthful, they soon picked up a nickname based on their peculiar uniform: the Blackshirts. Formed in 1922, the Blackshirts were the foot soldiers of the party. Blackshirt numbers grew to the point that at the beginning of the war, almost 40 legions of them were attached to the Italian army. Unlike many ordinary Italian troops, who showed little desire to fight, some Blackshirt regiments proved to be formidable opponents.

Blackshirt troops wore standard Italian army uniforms, but with black shirts and ties. Black collar patches bore the fasces badge of ancient Rome—a bundle of rods with the ax head—from which the fascists derived their name. They also carried a special dagger.

OTHER AXIS COUNTRIES

There were a few smaller members of the Axis powers, notably Romania, Hungary, and Finland, whose troops mainly saw action on the Russian front. Finnish troops wore a light gray uniform similar in style to the Germans', including the helmet, dice-shaker boots, leather webbing, and ski caps. The most obvious differences were badges, rank insignia, and the absence of the eagle and swastika. Hungarian uniform was also similar, but in khaki. Earlier in the

This Japanese infantryman is wearing a tropical uniform, without his single-breasted tunic, as often happened in the jungle heat. The field cap was common to all ranks.

Unusually, this Romanian infantryman, in 1945, seems to be wearing no badges or insignia. In a throwback to earlier wars, he is carrying a rolled blanket over his shoulder.

conflict, tall, dice-shaker boots were used, but ankle boots later became common. These showed the pantaloons, which were fitted with buttons that enabled them to be worn close to the calf. A side cap, large greatcoat, and brown leather webbing completed the outfit. Once again, their main distinguishing marks, apart from the color, were their insignia.

Romanian dress was the most distinctive. Other ranks' uniforms were in khaki, and comprised a short tunic and pantaloons worn with puttees, or trousers worn with anklets. The anklets were in brown leather, as were the webbing and ankle boots. The uniform was finished off with a ski cap and greatcoat. The greatcoat, being unpadded, gave little protection against the extreme cold of the Eastern front, and many Romanian troops literally froze to death. The most distinctive piece of their uniform was the large Dutch steel helmet, which looked like a metal pith helmet.

Romanian officers were better dressed, similar to the style of U.S. officers, with khaki breeches, a deeper brown, single-breasted, four-pocket tunic, worn with a Sam Browne-style belt over a light khaki shirt and darker brown tie. Tall leather riding boots might be worn, or puttees and ankle boots. The cap would be the normal officers' peaked cap.

CHAPTER 4

Uniforms Since 1945

After World War II, newly independent nations with armies of their own modeled their uniforms on those of such countries as Britain and the United States, but conflicts in various parts of the world required further modifications to suit function and climate.

Millions of men had been called upon to fight in World War II, and millions of uniforms, guns, and items of equipment had been produced for them. When the war ended, these were returned to the **stores**, while the vast majority of soldiers went back to civilian life.

This private of the Chinese People's Liberation Army in the Korean War is wearing a quilted coat and pants, with a fur hat for the bitter cold of the Korean winter. He has on old-fashioned puttees and what can best be described as slippers.

These U.S. troops are in camouflage coats and pants, with helmet covers. The bulging pockets on the jackets and pants, the pouches for items such as ammunition, and the grenade and machete give an indication of the personal kit carried.

These stores, and particularly those of Britain and the U.S., were sold to smaller countries all over the world. In Britain's case, this happened as part of the process of the dissolution of its empire. The British government had called on the peoples of the empire to provide troops to help in the war. The colonies had supplied literally millions of men, and now they wanted to be paid back—with independence. As this began to take place, the new countries needed armies, and these were clothed and supplied from British stocks. In many cases, they wore virtually the same uniforms that they had worn before achieving independence.

In the immediate postwar years, the armies of India, Pakistan, and many African and Middle Eastern countries dressed in basic British tropical uniforms; however, by the early 1950s, this changed when better-quality American equipment came onto the international market. This combination led to some strange situations. Israeli troops wore U.S. uniforms, so in the first Arab-Israeli war, American-dressed Israeli forces were facing British-dressed Arab forces. Stranger still, after the partition of India into India and Pakistan, troops facing each other across the border were all dressed in British uniforms.

Israeli paratroopers in the 1990s. The soldier in the center is wearing a ballistic nylon helmet and Kevlar body armor under his tunic, both of which give good protection against small-arms fire and shell splinters.

THE COLD WAR

A new type of war, the Cold War, was brewing between the West, led by the United States, and the Communist bloc, led by Russia. It was called "cold"

This U.S. infantryman is in an NBC (nuclear, biological, and chemical) suit. The suit, with its built-in gas mask, enables the wearer to operate in an environment that would otherwise be fatal. The powder is a part of the protection.

because it rarely became a shooting war between the main countries. Fighting usually occurred between smaller countries who were influenced by these two powerful countries. These were almost proxy wars, where the forces of the smaller countries were armed, and clothed, by their respective superpowers.

This proxy warfare meant a shift in the main theater of warfare, from Europe and North Africa, to Southeast Asia, starting with Vietnam, or French Indochina, as it was then called. There, the French, who had been forced out by the Japanese, tried to retake control from the largely Communist forces, who had fought an Allied-supported guerrilla action against the Japanese army and now wanted independence. Once again, the French forces wore a combination of American and British uniforms.

In 1951, North Korean forces, supported by **Red Chinese** troops, invaded the United Nations (UN)–backed South Korea, and the Korean War began. Unfortunately, the UN forces were not prepared for the severe winter conditions. The Communist forces, on the other hand, wore distinct uniforms that gave superior protection from the weather. This was in the form of light gray or brown, double-breasted jackets made of thickly quilted material (there were both long and waist-length versions) and trousers. Puttees might still be worn with them, as were thin sandals, although most wore boots when they could get them. Helmets were unusual among the Communist forces; they preferred caps with large earflaps to give protection from the bitter winds. Russian-style fur-lined hats were most popular.

Most of the UN and South Korean forces fell back on America's 1943-style uniform with its multilayered approach. Even British forces took to wearing the U.S. field jacket and overtrousers on top of their battle dress, because the former had a high degree of wind and rain protection. U.S. Arctic-issue caps with large earflaps were also popular; like the field jacket, they were made from wind- and rainproof material on the outside with a woolen lining.

This modern British soldier is in camouflage battle dress. His face is camouflaged, and his helmet has a camouflage cover, which has strips of material attached to the netting, in the same way as the large camouflage net behind.

Meanwhile, in Malaya, Britain was carrying on a war against Communist-backed **guerrillas** in different conditions. Here, it was hot, steamy jungle fighting, and these conditions dictated a different uniform. Troops here favored the bush hat, fatigue shirt, and waterproof trousers, all in olive green or khaki,

"HARD" AND "SOFT" ARMOR

Originally known as bulletproof vests, or flak jackets (the latter name springs from the garment issued to U.S. bomber crews to protect against German flak, or antiaircraft fire), body armor comes in two categories: soft and hard. Hard armor is the heavyweight variety used by bomb-disposal teams, using solid ceramic plates in an imitation of the breastplates of pre-20th–century cavalry. Hard armor can deflect even high-velocity bullets. Soft armor, on the other hand, is lighter and gives protection against low-velocity (pistol or submachine gun) ammunition. It does not always stop rifle rounds, but it does make the wounds they cause less serious.

worn with high, laced-up jungle boots made mostly of canvas (the wet conditions would rot leather boots in a few weeks). British uniforms, and the tactics they used, had been drawn from their experience against the Japanese in Burma, and would be drawn upon by Australian and U.S. troops in Vietnam.

THE VIETNAM WAR

The Vietnam War saw a great expansion in the use of some earlier innovations. The use of the bulletproof vest, or flak jacket, among U.S. troops became extremely widespread. In addition, camouflage was emerging with new patterns, such as the famous "tiger stripe," and there was a growth in the use of camouflage makeup for the face.

BODY ARMOR

Since Vietnam, the trend has been for smaller armies made up of multispecialist professional troops. Their training is intensive and expensive, and great emphasis is now placed on giving them as much protection as possible. This takes two main forms: body armor and nuclear, chemical, and biological warfare suits. Vietnam War-period flak jackets weighed a lot. They were fastened at the front with zippers and press studs, and in combat, this proved to be a weak spot if the jackets were not correctly fitted. Around the bottom of the flak jackets was a band of material fitted with eyelets, from which the wearer could hang equipment. In the 1980s, the Israelis expanded on this design by fitting ammunition and equipment pouches directly to their flak jackets. They were not the only piece of body armor; U.S. combat boots had a steel plate in the sole to protect against booby traps made of sharpened bamboo stakes.

Body armor poses the same problem as medieval plate armor. More armor gives more protection, but there is a trade-off: armor constricts movement, so more armor means less movement. What remains is a balancing act. Most modern jackets are designed to cover the wearer from neck to hips, leaving the arms and legs free. In this way, running and firing are not overly hampered, while the more serious targets—the head and chest—are protected by the helmet and the flak jacket.

Today's bulletproof vest is made from new synthetic materials, such as Kevlar, which are tough but light—6 to 11 pounds (2.7 to 5 kg) on average. To enable them to be put on and removed quickly—necessary in the case of surprise attack or for medical treatment—they use Velcro fittings, usually under the arms. This makes them easier to adjust to different sizes, while at the same time avoids the weak spot provided by the earlier front-fastening models. The new, lightweight materials mean that some are designed to be worn under a combat jacket, making it easier to get to all the gear packed in the combat jacket's pockets.

Several thin layers of bulletproof material provide far better protection than a single thick layer. The 1990s U.S. Army PASGT (personal armor system—ground troops) flak vest is made from several layers of Kevlar ballistic cloth over trauma-shield padding to protect the wearer from injuries created by the force of the bullet hitting the vest. Many countries' vests include pockets in the front and back for plates of additional hard armor to give extra protection. The American vest also features a high collar to protect the neck: this, together with the Kevlar helmet, creates a virtual shield that protects from the groin to the top of the head.

The modern helmet is no longer made of steel, but of layers of ballistic fiber, which, unlike its predecessor, will protect against small-arms fire. It, too, has a trauma lining and is made to fit over ear defenders, personal two-way radio, and night-vision sets.

NUCLEAR, BIOLOGICAL, AND CHEMICAL SUITS

Nuclear, biological, and chemical (NBC) suits are part of the individual protection equipment issued to the modern soldier. In the late 1960s, this consisted of a gas mask and a rubberized gas cape. These days, most troops carry two suits: one to wear, and one spare, made up of trousers, a smock (both with Velcro fasteners), overboots, and gloves. The whole suit is hot, sweaty, and

This officer of the 1990s Spanish Special Operations Group is wearing a one-piece combat coverall in Spanish camouflage, with cargo pockets, and a balaclava helmet.

uncomfortable to wear, but ultimately preferable to the alternative. The suit is completed by a gas mask that includes a microphone, optional air supply, and dark eyeglasses to protect against flash.

Other new uniform materials include fire-retarding fabrics, such as carbon fiber, for tank crews and special forces suits. The latter, usually in black, often incorporates special features, such as fire-retardant pads on the elbows and knees to allow the wearer to crawl over hot surfaces.

This Operation Desert Storm USAF soldier wears desert camouflage fatigues, including a slouch hat, in 1991. The darker webbing seems wrong, but the contrast is effective in breaking up his overall shape.

These suits and body armor are just a small part of the kit carried by modern soldiers. New weapons and equipment have meant an ever-increasing load for troops, which includes weapons, ammunition, **rations**, water, spare clothing, shelter, sleeping bag, NBC suit, first-aid kit, specialist equipment, personal kit, and much more. Improved carrying systems and webbing have meant that the weight can be better distributed, but the load can be as much as 100 pounds (45 kg), a substantial increase from the 70 pounds (32 kg) carried by their great-grandfathers in World War I.

CONCLUSION

Uniform design has been influenced by changes—technical, social, and scientific—throughout the last century. Industrialization and the need to equip huge armies led to standardization. More efficient weapons led to the end of bright colors and the introduction of khaki and other drab colors, while shelling resurrected the steel helmet, and gas masks were introduced to counter certain chemical weapons.

By World War II, standardization gave way to uniforms tailored to meet the needs of different specialist units, while the use of camouflage, introduced by the German army, became widespread throughout the world. The 1943 U.S. uniform led the way in introducing the idea of a uniform made up of several layers of thin, weatherproof cloth, while the first experiments in the use of the bulletproof vest were made.

The end of the century saw the introduction of the specialist professional soldier, prepared for the use of gas, biological, or nuclear warfare. Levels of personal protection were hugely increased in the form of flak jackets, NBC suits, and the use of flame-retardant materials and Kevlar helmets.

At present, experiments with high technology in the form of night-vision goggles, personal computers, and personal radar are leading the way to the creation of a super soldier. Work on materials that can self-camouflage or cut down the wearer's body-heat emissions to make them invisible to infrared is pointing the way to a whole new generation of uniforms. More and more women are now serving in the armed forces on equal terms with their male colleagues and, as such, they are wearing the same uniforms and carrying the same equipment.

When looking back over the century, from the cavalry regiments with their bright, gold-braided uniforms, swords, and shining helmets, to the ultracamouflaged, high-tech super-warrior of today, it is fascinating to imagine what directions the uniforms of the 21st century will take.

GLOSSARY

Anklet a covering for the ankle, buckled or buttoned at the side

Anorak a pullover hooded jacket long enough to cover the hips

Balaclava helmet knitted, close-fitting hood with a hole for the face, like a ski mask

Battle dress uniform for combat use

Bayonet a knife that can be attached to a rifle

Beret a visorless, usually woolen, cap with a tight headband and a soft, full, flat top

Blouson short jacket, usually waist-length, often gathered

Breastplate piece of armor covering the chest

Bush hat a fabric hat with a wide brim, or shaped like a baseball cap with a shade at the front

Camouflage pattern designed to blend in with its surroundings

Campaign hat brimmed, cowboy-style hat

Chain mail armor made from small interlocking rings

Collar patch cloth badge worn on the collar

Commonwealth an association of self-governing autonomous states more or less loosely associated in a common allegiance

Conscript a military recruit

Conscription compulsory enrollment of persons, especially for military service

Cosh a weighted weapon similar to a blackjack

Dressings material applied to cover a wound

Dungaree blue denim

Edelweiss a small alpine plant

Epaulet an ornamental strip or loop sewn across the shoulder of a dress or coat

Eyelet a small hole designed to receive a cord or used for decoration

Farrier a person who shoes horses

Fascist a person who believes in centralized autocratic government headed by a dictatorial leader, severe economic and social regimentation, and forcible suppression of opposition

Fatigues the uniform or work clothing worn on fatigue (or working) and in the field

Forage cap an infantry undress cap

Grenadier a soldier who uses grenades

Guerrilla a person who engages in irregular warfare, especially as a member of an independent unit carrying out harassment and sabotage

Gurkha Nepalese soldier serving in the British army

Herringbone a pattern of parallel lines, with adjacent rows sloping in opposite directions

Ike jacket U.S. blouson jacket, named after General Dwight D. Eisenhower

Insignia badges

Jerkin sleeveless overjacket, usually leather

Jodhpurs riding breeches, wide around the thighs, then skintight from the knees

Kapok a mass of silky fibers used as a filling for mattresses, sleeping bags, and as insulation

Khaki a dull brown-yellow color

Kilt a knee-length pleated skirt, usually of tartan, worn by Scottish men

Kukris a curved Nepalese dagger

Lance a spear used by cavalry

Luftwaffe the first German air force

Noncommissioned rank any rank above that of private, but not officers

Pantaloons loose trousers gathered at the knee

Peaked cap cap with peak, as worn by police

Pip a diamond-shaped rank badge, used in the German and British armies

Pith helmet a lightweight helmet-shaped hat made of pith or cork

Poncho a sleeveless, waterproof garment slipped over the head

Pork pie cap similar to a peaked cap but without the peak

Pouch pocket pocket sewn onto the outside of a garment

Rations a food allowance for one day

Red Chinese Communist Chinese

Sam Browne belt officer's belt with a diagonal supporting strap

Side cap cap that can be folded flat, such as Boy Scouts wear

Singlet a sleeveless undershirt

Ski cap soft cap with a peak; worn by mountain troops

Skullcap a close-fitting cap

Slouch hat hat with a large, floppy brim

Spats a cloth or leather gaiter covering the instep and ankle

Store supplies

Tam-o'-shanter a woolen cap of Scottish origin with a headband, wide flat circular crown, and a pompon in the center

Tropical kit uniform for use in hot climates

Tunic military jacket

walking out dress order of dress worn off duty

webbing straps attached to the belt, going over the shoulders, to help carry equipment.

TIMELINE

1914 The Great War (World War I) begins.

1915 First use of poison gas by Germany; first gas masks.

1916 First use of the tank by Great Britain.

1917 U.S. enters the Great War; the Women's Auxiliary Army Corps is founded in

Britain; steel helmets introduced by many countries; first use of camouflage painting on helmets by Germany.

1918 The end of the Great War.

1927 First military parachute unit formed by Italy.

1929 First use of camouflage cloth for tents by Italy.

1930 First camouflage cloth for clothing—a poncho—by Germany.

1935 Hitler announces the reintroduction of conscription in Germany.

1939 World War II breaks out in Europe.

1940 British troops use winter camouflage.

1941 U.S. enters World War II; introduction of new U.S. helmet.

1943 U.S. Army introduces new uniform designs.

1945 First atomic bombs; end of World War II; birth of the United Nations.

1947 First use of the term "Cold War."

1948 Two Korean states established (North and South); first Arab-Israeli war.

1950 North Korean forces invade the South, starting the Korean War.

1953 Korean armistice signed.

1954 Guerrilla warfare begins between South Vietnamese army and Communist Viet Cong.

1959 North Vietnamese troops join in conflict in South Vietnam.

1961 U.S. troops sent to Vietnam.

1967 Six Day War between Arabs and Israelis.

1973 Yom Kippur War between Arabs and Israelis; U.S. troops pull out of Vietnam.

1975 End of Vietnam War.

1982 Falklands War between Great Britain and Argentina.

1991 Gulf War.

FURTHER INFORMATION

BOOKS

Bull, Stephen. *World War One.* London: Brassey's, 1998.

Cormack, Andrew. *British Air Forces. Vols. 1 and 2, 1914–18.* Oxford: Osprey Military, 2001.

Chappell, Mike. *Scottish Units in the World Wars.* London: Osprey, 1994.

Davis, Brian. *British Army Uniforms and Insignia of World War Two.* London: Arms and Armour Press, 1992.

Gavin, Lettie. *American Women in World War I*. Niwot, Colo.: Colorado University Press, 1983.

Mollo, Andrew. *Armed Forces of World War II*. London: Orbis, 1981.

Sumner, Ian. *The Indian Army 1914–1947*. Oxford: Osprey, 2001.

Sumner, Ian, François Vauvillier, and Mike Chappell. *The French Army 1939–1945*. Vol 1. London: Osprey Military, 1998.

ONLINE SOURCES

Military Uniform Prints

http://www.military-uniforms.com

Dedicated to military uniform plates from ancient times to modern armed forces, this site does not provide much written information, but is a great visual reference.

Military Uniforms

http://militaryhistory.about.com/cs/militaryuniforms

This page provides a good range of links to others sites devoted to specific types of uniforms.

ABOUT THE AUTHORS

Mike Brown lives in London, England, where he writes part-time and teaches part-time, in addition to giving talks and lectures on 20th-century history and architecture to a wide range of audiences, from primary schools to retirement groups. He has written a book on Britain's Civil Defence Services in World War II, *Put That Light Out,* published in 2000. Other books include *A Child's War,* and, in conjunction with his wife, Carol Harris, *The Wartime House.*

Carol Harris is a freelance journalist and lecturer specializing in the 1920s, 1930s, and 1940s. She has contributed to exhibitions at the Imperial War Museum on wartime fashions and utility clothing, and she regularly gives talks on these and related topics. Her other books include *Collecting Twentieth-Century Fashion and Accessories* (Mitchell Beazley 1999), *Women at War—the Home Front* (Sutton, 2001), and *Women at War—in Uniform* (Sutton, 2002).

INDEX